Shop Till You Drop

John Goodwin

Published in association with
The Basic Skills Agency

Hodder Murray

A MEMBER OF THE HODDER HEADLINE GROUP

Hachette's policy is to use papers that are natural, renewable
and recyclable products and made from wood grown in sustainable
forests. The logging and manufacturing processes are expected to
conform to the environmental regulations of the country of origin.

Orders: please contact Bookpoint Ltd, 130 Milton Park, Abingdon, Oxon
OX14 4SB. Telephone: (44) 01235 827720. Fax: (44) 01235 400454. Lines are
open from 9.00am to 5.00pm, Monday to Saturday, with a 24-hour
message answering service.
Visit our website at www.hoddereducation.co.uk

© John Goodwin 2000, 2006
First published in the Livewire series in 2000 and first published in the
Hodder Reading Project series in 2006 by Hodder Education,
Hachette UK company, 338 Euston Road, London NW1 3BH.

Impression number   10 9 8 7
Year   2011

All rights reserved. Apart from any use permitted under UK copyright
law, no part of this publication may be reproduced or transmitted in any
form or by any means, electronic or mechanical, including photocopying
and recording, or held within any information storage and retrieval
system, without permission in writing from the publisher or under
licence from the Copyright Licensing Agency Limited. Further details of
such licences (for reprographic reproduction) may be obtained from the
Copyright Licensing Agency Limited, Saffron House, 6-10 Kirby Street,
London EC1N 8TS.

Cover photo: Shopping bags © Big Cheese Photo LLC/Alamy.
Internal artwork © Gary Andrews.
Typeset by Transet Ltd, Coventry, England.
Printed and bound by CPI Group (UK) Ltd, Croydon, CR0 4YY

A catalogue record for this title is available from the British Library

ISBN 978 0 340 91568 4

Contents

		Page
1	Jez	1
2	A New Image	3
3	Shopping	7
4	The Credit Card	11
5	New Clothes	14
6	The Post	18
7	'Oh Lucy'	21
8	The School Party	27

1
Jez

'Jez fancies you, Lucy,' said Jenna.

'Jez?'

'Yeah,' said Jenna.

'How do you know?' I asked.

'He's been asking about you.
What you're like.
Where you live.
That sort of stuff.'

I could feel myself going red.
'What did you tell him?' I asked.

'Not much,' she said.
'It's best if he finds out for himself,
isn't it?'

My face was on fire.
Jez Cooper fancied me,
Lucy Snedden.
Wow.
I don't fancy him.
He's a bit of a prat,
but I'm pleased he fancies me.
Pleased to bits.

2

A New Image

Snip.
A curl of my hair fell to the ground.
Clip.
Two curls of hair fell down.
Cut, snip, clip.

'Steady on, Jenna,' I cried.

'Relax, Lucy.
Sit back in your chair.
You're going to look so cool,'
said Jenna.

'I don't want it too short,' I said.

Jenna cut away.
More of my hair fell to the ground.
A minute later she'd finished.
'Now you can look in the mirror,'
she said.

I opened one eye and then the other.
A new me with spiky hair
was clear to see.

'It's a bit short,' I said.

'It's amazing,' said Jenna.
'You wanted a new image,
and now you've got one.
Jez will love it.'

'Will he?' I asked.

'Oh yeah,' said Jenna.
'You just wait and see.'

Next day at school I smiled at Jez.
'Hi,' I said.
Jez didn't smile back or grin at me.
Instead, he looked away and ran off.
'My hair is a disaster,' I told Jenna.

'No, no,' she said.
'Your hair is wicked.
You just need some new clothes.

You need a new style
to go with your new hair.
Then Jez will go wild about you.'

'Will he?'

'Oh yeah. You wait and see,'
said Jenna.

It was fine for Jenna to talk
about new clothes,
and to say I needed a new style.
It was great for her to tell me that Jez
would go wild about me.
A new image doesn't come cheap.
How was I ever going to get any cash
to buy new stuff?

3
Shopping

I looked at myself in the mirror.
It was a long full mirror.
I could see myself from top to toe.
My clothes were fine.
They felt comfortable.
They weren't new.
They weren't cool.
They were a bit baggy maybe.
But they were me.
I felt good in them.

Jenna came round and we went into town.
'I haven't any cash to buy anything,'
I told her.
Jenna goes to town every Saturday.
She loves shopping
and she shops big time.
Most Saturdays I go swimming
with my brother.
Blue water splashing in my face
gave way to busy streets
and crowded shops.

Jenna was on a mission.
It was serious shopping time.
'Try this on, Lucy,' she said,
grabbing a jacket from the clothes rack.

'There's no point.
I don't have any cash,' I said.

'And this … and this,' she said.
She wasn't listening to what I was saying.

She pushed a bundle of clothes
into my hands.
'Go to the fitting room.
Try them on,' she said.

I pushed them back towards her.
'I told you that I don't have any money.'

'Relax,' she said.
'Just try them on.
Nobody says you have to buy them.
It's only a bit of a giggle.'

Three minutes later I was back
by her side.
'That was quick,' she said.

'No good,' I lied.
'The jacket didn't fit and the trousers
made my bum look huge.
A total waste of time,' I told her.

Back at home I looked at myself
in the mirror again.
I wasn't comfortable any longer.
My jeans looked old and tatty.
My sweat-shirt was ripped and frayed.
I ran my hands over my shoulders.
I could still feel the sleek smoothness
of the jacket in the shop.
So trim.
So cool.
I had to have it.

4

The Credit Card

I held up the store credit card.
It had been stuffed in a drawer for ages.
Mum had never used it.
I turned it over in my hand.
It wasn't even signed.
I could get the jacket with that card.
It would just be the jacket –
nothing else.
I could pay Mum back later.
That was the moment when
my hand reached out for a pen.

I went to town after school,
on my own.
I changed out of my school uniform
in the ladies toilet.
I put on some make-up.
Anyone might think I was 18,
and old enough to have
my own credit card.

The jacket was still on the rack.
There was just one left in my size.
My hand felt into my pocket.
My fingers gripped the edges
of the neat plastic shape.
It was so simple.
I lifted the jacket clear of the rack
and turned towards the till.

'Hello, Lucy,' said a familiar voice.
I froze.
'Smart jacket you've got there.'
Jenna reached out to stroke it.

'You'll look a stunner
at the school party wearing that.
All the lads will fancy you.
You wait and see.'

At the cash till the woman
didn't even look at me.
I showed her the card
and signed with my mum's name.

'The boys won't be ignoring you now,'
said Jenna. 'You'll look like a star.'

5

New Clothes

It wasn't enough.
The jacket looked cool, for sure.
It was a neat and sleek fit,
but the rest of my clothes were dreadful.
I couldn't go to a party in them.
No way.
I had to be a star.
I wanted to see all the lads staring at me.
I needed more new clothes.
I needed them until it hurt.

Shoes, jeans, socks.
Knitwear, silkwear, anywear.
Silky, shiny clothes.
Chunky, bobbly clothes.
There were clothes that fitted,
and others that didn't.
I bought the lot.

With slippery plastic carriers,
at least one in each hand,
I joined the throng of shoppers.
I danced down the streets.
I drank in the bright lights.
I gobbled up the buzz.
'Shop till you drop,
and then shop again.'
I was alive.

I had to wait until my mum was out
before I could bring my shopping home.
Then I got more daring.
I'd hear her in the kitchen
and sneak upstairs.
I'd climb up the stairs and make sure
I didn't tread on the creaking stair.
I'd lock my bedroom door behind me.
I'd stuff it all in my wardrobe,
until it was overflowing.
I'd hide it under my bed.
A secret is safe when it's hidden away.

One day I wore a silky new top to school.
I hid it under my jacket when I left home.
When I walked into the classroom
all the lads stared.
Jez and Ben and Zak and Tariq,
they all had their mouths wide open.
Their chins practically bounced
off their work tables.

'That's not school uniform, Lucy.
Put your jacket back on immediately.'

Why do teachers have to spoil
everything?
I had my jacket off
for less than five minutes,
but it was worth it.
It was worth every single second.

'Jez really does fancy you, Lucy,'
said Jenna.

'I know,' I replied.

'So do Ben, Zak and Tariq,' said Jenna.

I beamed a huge smile.
It lasted the rest of the day.

6

The Post

My mum was out when the post came.
She had two letters addressed to her.
I picked them both up off the floor
where they'd landed.
I wished I hadn't touched them.
I recognised the logo
on one of the letters.
It was the same logo that was
on the store credit card.
It was in a bright red colour.
Too bright.
Fire bright.
It was burning in my hand.

For ages I stood holding the letters.
I couldn't move.
I was unsure what to do next.
I put my fingernail under the corner
of the flap of the logo letter.
With just one flick I could open it
and see what was inside.
I could read how much I'd spent.
My fingernail was sharp,
but my brain was dull.

I lurched into the kitchen
and put one letter on the table.
I ripped the second into pieces.
Then ripped the pieces into tiny bits.
But the red brightness still shone out.
I raced into the lounge
and set fire to the bits in the fire grate.
The flames turned them all to grey ash.
I banged the poker on the ash
until it was dust.

7

'Oh Lucy'

It was the week of the school party.
Jenna and I were up in my bedroom.
We were trying on a load of clothes
that we might wear at the party.
We were having a real giggle.
We had music turned up loud –
wall to wall sound.

'What about these?' shouted Jenna
waving a pair of silky black trousers.

'Too tight,' I shouted back louder.

Then Jenna grabbed a very sparkly top.
'Oh Lucy,' she shouted.
'You must wear this.
You'll be so cool.
Try it on so I can see
what you look like.'

Before I could take the top from her
there was a shout from downstairs.
'Lucy,' called Mum.

Jenna turned the music up even louder
and began to dance about.
She was holding the sparkly top
as if she was dancing with it.
Mum shouted again.
'Lucy, I need to speak to you.'
The music almost drowned her out –
nearly, but not quite.
There was something strange
about her voice.

A few seconds later
I closed my bedroom door behind me.
I went downstairs.
Mum was standing
with a letter in her hand.
'We need to talk, Lucy,' she said.

Jenna went home.
The music stopped.

Mum was looking me in the eyes.
'Have you been shopping?' she said.
'Did you use that old store credit card?
This letter has just come.
Is this anything to do with you?'

She put the letter into my hands.
It was the credit card bill, for £567.24.

For a minute I was going to lie
and say that I knew nothing about it.

I'd tell her that there must
be some mistake.
I'd tell her that
they'd got the wrong address.
Then I saw Mum's face and I knew
I had to tell her everything.

'These are things you've bought,
aren't they?' she said.
I nodded.
'Oh Lucy,' she said.
'How could you have done such a thing?'

'I'm sorry,' I stammered.

'Why didn't you tell me about it?'
she said.
I opened my mouth
but no words came out.
'I can never pay this bill,' she said.
'I simply don't have the money.'

8

The School Party

I sit looking out of the window
at the black sky.
It's the night of the school party.
Jenna will be dancing.
Jez will be laughing.
Maybe he'll be dancing too.
And Ben and Zak and Tariq
will be having a really wicked time.

Jenna said I must go.
She said it didn't matter
if I didn't have anything special to wear.
She even offered to lend me
some of her clothes.

My bedroom is empty.
All the new clothes have been sent
back to the shop.
Mum is still worrying
about the credit card bill.
Nothing has been finally sorted.
She may have to pay back some of it.

And me?
I'd sooner not talk about it.
Let's just say
I won't be shopping for a while.

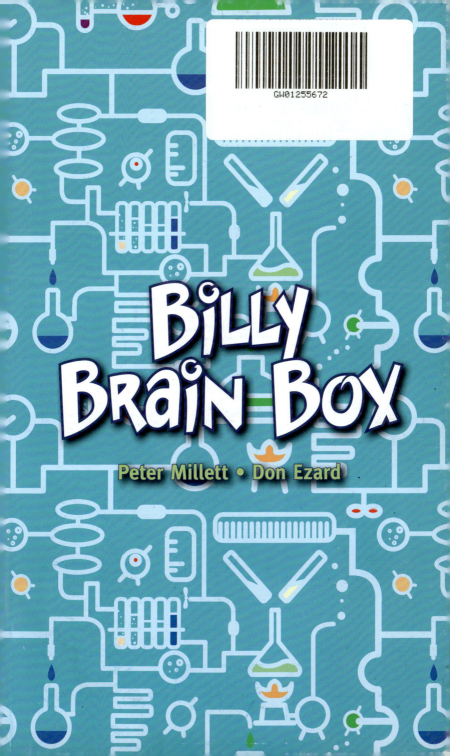

Billy Brain Box

Written by Peter Millett • Illustrated by Don Ezard

© 2012 Macmillan Education Australia Pty Ltd

All rights reserved. No part of this publication may be reproduced, stored in a retrieval system, or transmitted in any form or by any means, electronic, mechanical, photocopying, recording, or otherwise, without the prior permission of the copyright owner. While every care has been taken to trace and acknowledge copyright, the publishers tender their apologies for any accidental infringement where copyright has proved untraceable.

Published by
Macmillan Education Australia Pty Ltd
Level 1, 15–19 Claremont Street, South Yarra,
Victoria 3141
www.macmillan.com.au

Edited by Janne Galbraith and Berit Bolstad
Designed by Andrew Aguilar

Printed in China
10 9 8 7 6 5 4 3 2 1

ISBN: 978-1-4202-9775-1 (pack)
978-1-4202-9754-6

Contents

1 A Happy Accident. 7

2 Chore Time 11

3 A Barrel of Paint. 15

4 An Intruder at Large. 18

5 Invisible Footprints 23

6 Billy Saves the Day. 28

Author. 30

Illustrator. 31

Read More Sprints 32

Characters

Hi! I´m Billy Brain Box. I like inventing all kinds of gadgets and gizmos!

Hello, I´m Billy Brain Box´s gran. My grandson is the smartest boy in the world!

OUTWOODS EDGE PRIMARY SCHOOL
21 Redwood Road Loughborough

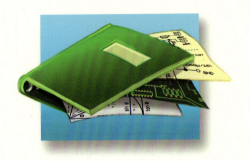

Chapter 1

A Happy Accident

Hi, my name is William. You can call me Bill if you like. That's what Mum and Dad call me. My sister does, too, but my gran calls me Billy Brain Box. She thinks my inventions are **super-brainy**. The **trouble** is, nobody else does!

My latest invention is invisible paint. How did I invent invisible paint? **Easy**! It was an accident.

I was mixing some invisible ink to use as a prank on my sister. Suddenly, I sneezed really hard. **Ah-choo**! **Ah-choo**! **Ah-choo**! The force of my sneezes knocked the invisible ink bottle off the table. It fell into a bucket of lemon juice Mum had squeezed for lemonade.

I recovered from my sneezing fit and glanced down. To my **surprise**, I saw that the bucket was gone!

"Oh, no!" I cried. "Where did my bucket go?"

The bucket wasn't really gone. It was still there. It had been made invisible by the liquid inside. I kicked it with my foot. **Ouch**! A splash landed on my shoe. My shoe disappeared!

"**Whoa**! Invisible paint!" I said.

Chapter 2

CHORE TIME

"Hi, Bill. What's up?" Mum asked as I walked outside with the invisible bucket.

"I've just invented invisible paint!" I said.

"Really?" Mum answered. "Where is it?"

"Right here," I said. I held the invisible bucket up in the air. "You can't see it. It's invisible!"

Mum didn't believe me. "You and your **imagination**!" she laughed.

Later that day, I showed Dad my bucket of invisible paint. He looked at me as if I was **crazy**. Then, he told me to get on with weeding the garden. **Boring**!

"I wish the weeds in our garden would disappear forever!" I cried.

Then, I had a **brilliant** idea. I would make the weeds disappear with my new invisible paint!

I grabbed a brush and started painting the weeds. They were all gone in five minutes. **Cool**!

Later, Mum asked me to tidy my room. I **HATE** picking up stuff. So, I painted it all away with my invisible paint! My room was tidy in two minutes. This was my **coolest** invention ever!

Chapter 3

A Barrel of Paint

I rushed back to the shed to mix more invisible paint. I'd need plenty. Dad had a **million** chores lined up for me, and I planned to paint them all away. I also wanted to take some paint to school. It would make my maths problems disappear.

I put the ingredients in a big old wooden barrel. I mixed them up with Dad's old rake. All the stirring made it disappear. **Whoops!** I hoped Dad wouldn't miss it.

I got up early the next morning. I couldn't wait to start "painting out" my chores. I went to the shed to grab the paint and a brush. But when I got there, I saw that all the paint was **GONE**! The barrel had been knocked over. All the invisible paint had spilled out!

"**Oh, no!**" I cried.

Chapter 4

An Intruder at Large

The paint wasn't the only thing missing. My sister's skateboard had disappeared. So had my brand-new bike.

Gran waved at me from over the fence.

"Billy, my garden hose is gone!" she cried. "And Grandad's new lawnmower, too. We must have had an intruder last night."

"An intruder?" I growled. "I can't stand intruders. They're WORSE than garden weeds!"

"Billy Brain Box, you must use your **clever** brain to solve this crime," Gran said. "Grandad wants his lawnmower back! He's very *upset*. It's like a friend to him."

I heaved the empty barrel up into place. Another **brilliant** thought popped into my head. Whoever had come into the shed must have **knocked** over my barrel of invisible paint. The intruder must have walked through the paint to reach my bike. They must have left a trail of invisible footprints. Those footprints would lead us straight to the thief! **Wow**! I felt like some kind of weed-hating, crime-busting detective.

"Gran, I think I know how to solve this crime!" I said. I grabbed my invisible ink reading lamp. "Follow me," I said to Gran. "Let's find Grandad's friend!"

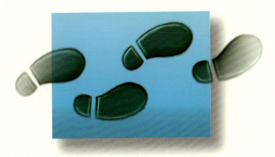

Chapter 5

Invisible Footprints

I **shined** the lamp around the shed. **STRANGE** footprints appeared. They led out of the shed, through the garden, and into Gran's. Then, they went down the road. We followed the footprints until they led us to the door of an old house. "Gran!" I said. "Call the police!"

As Gran dialled the number, I noticed that my lamp was flickering oddly. I shook it hard, but that turned out to be a bad idea.

With a fizz and a pop, the lamp died. The visible footprints became invisible again. "Oh, no!" I cried. With a groan, I tossed it aside.

When the police arrived, I tried to explain about the invisible footprints. They looked at me as if I was crazy.

The police were more interested in a man who was staring curiously out the window of the house. He turned pale when he saw them, too! It turns out that he was well known in police circles. Once they'd arrested him, they found all the **stolen** goods inside his house.

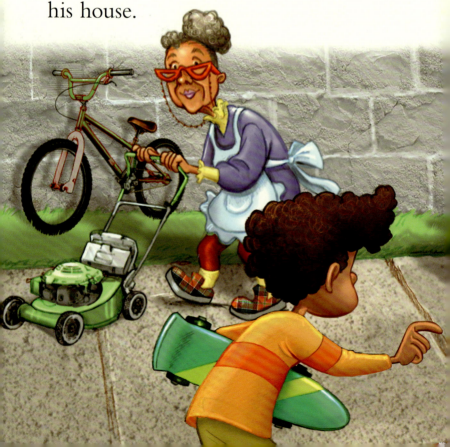

The police thought it was odd that the thief was barefoot. Why wouldn't they believe me when I told them about his invisible shoes?

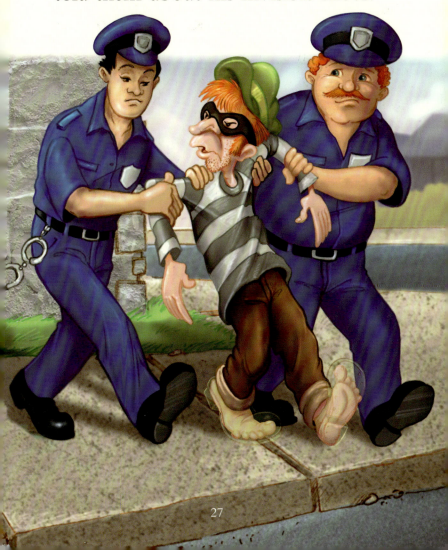

Chapter 6

Billy Saves the Day

When we got home, Gran baked me a **special** cake. She was the only one who believed my story about the invisible paint.

"Well done, Billy Brain Box! You **SAVED** the day!" she cheered.

Mum and Dad gave me a reward for tracking down the thief. It was a new rake to replace the one that had disappeared. "Now you can do your chores again, son!" said Dad.

To this day, they still don't believe me about the invisible paint. But one day I'll prove it. Perhaps I'll mix up another batch…

AUTHOR

Peter Millett lives in Auckland, New Zealand. He was nine years old when one of his poems appeared in the local newspaper. He has gone on to write a great many children's books. His favourite author is Roald Dahl.

Peter spends his time thinking up story ideas with his two children. His goal is to write books that are so funny you have a coughing fit when you're laughing out loud.

Illustrator

Don Ezard has always drawn and painted. His background is in 2D animation, illustration, design, and computer graphics. He enjoyed designing characters for two fun feature films, *Happy Feet* and *Legend of the Guardians: The Owls of Ga´Hoole*. As a matter of fact, penguins and owls are his favourite animals to draw!